The

Moon

Taught

Me

MARINE ASHNALIKYAN

The
Moon
Taught
Me

I write to fulfill one of God's callings on my life. I write to express myself and the world around me. I write to portray the beauty in humanity through our shared experiences. We love, we break. We face darkness. We search for the light. And if you are lucky, as I have been, you will face your "dark night of the soul." It will force you to find the light. It will force you to come face to face with your Creator. To find out who you are. To enter your Awakening.

I breathe life into this book. My life. My stories. I hope that with each page, and with each breath, you are inspired to look deep within. I hope you are inspired to be honest with yourself. To gain more understanding of who you are. And I hope you gain the courage to pursue the purpose for which you have been created.

For all you dreamers,

May you enter your Awakening and
make your dreams come to life.

"Whoever you are, now I place my hand upon

you, that you be my poem,

I whisper with my lips close to your ear,

I have loved many women and men, but I love

none better than you."

Walt Whitman

The Moon Taught Me

©2021 Marine Ashnalikyan

print ISBN: 978-1-09836-811-1
ebook ISBN: 978-1-09836-812-8

CONTENTS

The Heart

It feels. It loves. It breaks. It heals. Its very beat gives us life.

Without the heart, without love, there is no life.

My intuition is my compass—
I feel the vibrations of the Earth
beneath my feet,
I feel energy in the air,
they tell me
what will come to be.
Fire and water wage war
inside me—
I was right about everything
except you.

There was no tenderness
just yearning
and the enchantment of youth.

-first love

A handsome man
sitting next to me—
even then
I think of you.

I can have any
king in the deck,
but I only want you.

I can't tell if you're
the love of my life
or my muse.

The rain reminds me
of my childhood—
dancing outside with friends
with no care of the dew
that stained our clothes,
the rain reminds me of
Pride and Prejudice,
when Darcey told Elizabeth
she had bewitched him body and soul—
the rain reminds me of you.

When I look at
the stars,
I see your face—
brilliant and far away.

I've been Noah from
The Notebook
with overgrown hair
and a blank stare
filling your void
with people I don't love,
building the life
that was supposed to be ours,
hoping one day
it would lead you back home.

The fog hides
what's right in front of us—
love does that too.

Attached

Thanks to Levine and Heller's Attachment Theory, I learned that there are three types of attachment in relationships—secure, anxious, and avoidant. Most people have a secure attachment system. They are stable. People with anxious attachment have keen intuition. They feel deeply. They notice minute changes in their partner's demeanor. They can't let go until all the cells in their bodies decide, *I don't need this person anymore.* Avoidants run from intimacy. They're detached emotionally and numb to pain. No wonder. It's been years. I'm anxious. He's avoidant.

It's been so long
I can't remember
your face—
I listen to our song
over and over.

The hardest addiction
to overcome—
people.

I don't know
how many hearts
I have broken
without thinking twice—
you were my karma.

Even in my dreams
he tells me
he's not the one.

We don't have
a song—
every song
reminds me of you.

I drive for miles
to look at the rolling hills,

waste my time walking
on the ocean's shore,

paint the changing sunsets
of each day,

stare at the stars
for hours each night—

everything is a distraction
from you.

When you and I were over,
a million stars in the sky
stopped shining—
dreams died with us.

The truth about
everybody else—
they're not you.

My weakness
was loving you
before
loving myself.

I want a love
I can sit with
in silence
under the stars
and pretend like
we can comprehend
how beautiful
this world is.

You came like a storm—
unapologetic,
and without any doubt
if you belonged.

When we met,
I knew
I had loved you
for many lifetimes.

It was that combination
of gentle and wild
that made me
mad for you.

Only the moon
knows all the secrets
I tell her
about you.

Your love is warm
like the sun—
I feel it all over my skin.

When I'm with you
I'm transported to
a different place—
the sun is always bright,
and the world is royal blue.

Blue birds sing by the bay—
they tell the stories of us.

We all break
our rules
for love.

I'll see your darkness
and love you anyway.

The Dark

The void. The beginning. The place to start over.

When there was darkness, God created.

If I could go back in time,
I would go all the way
to the beginning—
when there was nothing
but darkness and God.

As a child, I heard
a man say to his wife,
I'm going to slaughter you,
and I thought,
this is what husbands do.

I can't un-feel it,
the trauma—
it's in my blood.

Grief

You make my body hurt
You have no grace
You put me to sleep—
the only way to forget.

Neighbors from Childhood

The friend I called Sister
for twenty-five years,
the old lady who babysat me
whose husband had Parkinson's disease,
the drug addict next door
that would chase his mom,
the woman that had her three-year-old son
wait outside on the nights
she conducted business,
and the pastor that baptized me.

I can't sleep between the hours
of midnight and 3 a.m.
I worry that if I do,
something bad will happen
and I won't be able to protect myself.

When I was a child, I slept with the covers
all the way up to my neck.
I thought if the monsters couldn't see me,
then they wouldn't be able to touch me.
I still sleep with the covers up to my neck.

She said, close your eyes,
Float above yourself
Go back to your ancestors—
What do you see—
Darkness.

Armenian Genocide

The first genocide of the 20th century
is the reason the word *genocide* was coined.

They say it's important to know history,
otherwise it repeats itself.

Hitler was inspired by the brutality
of the Ottoman Empire—

He said, *who after all speaks today
of the annihilation of the Armenians?*

My spirit is sad—
I carry the tears
of my ancestors.

I asked God
to teach me
how to forgive
the Turks
that killed, raped,
and displaced
Armenians—
then I looked up
and asked God
if he forgave
the devil.

Worn Out of War

Black smoke
shuts up the sky,
and makes its way into
people's lungs.

Out of the little boy's nose, eyes, mouth—
black liquids and the words,
Mommy, I don't ever
want to learn to speak.

A woman uses her hands
speaks no more
her two sons
tortured to death in front of her.

The land covered with oil,
black bubbling
black from the poison
they are forced to inhale.

My Dream about a Monkey and a Man

Racism is a man's gravest threat to man—
the maximum of hatred for a minimum of reason.

-Abraham Joshua Heschel

Monkeys and goats
fill the freeways—
bad traffic.

My professor from
Post-Colonial Theory
tries to move them away.

I want to get to my car
but a monkey hovers around it,
then turns into a man.

Professor McClintock says
he's a hybrid, not entirely ape,
not entirely human;

part street beggar, part gentleman.
Two strangers in black suits
watch him.

They tell me he'll attack
if I go near my car,
that he'll punch as hard as he can.

Why is *white*
always portrayed as good
and black as bad
when White colonizes
when White oppresses,
silences, and schemes—
when *White*
is the darkest of them all

-*White Supremacy*

The sadness in my body
makes it hard to get up
makes it hard to move
makes me slow,
makes me mad.

There are books and studies on the effects of heartbreak. Losing a loved one. Losing a job. But no one talks about losing a friend. A best friend. There are no books to help when you lose the one you called, *Sister*.

I lost my best friends
my savings
family members
and now you—
I didn't think
it would be you.

You keep breaking
my heart
as if you didn't know
it was already broken.

Around you, I always felt
like I was on trial—
like anything I said and did
could and would be used against me.

I had a dream
I was hitting you,

I slapped and pushed you,
threw sunflower seeds on you,

but you just stood there—
no reaction.

-the opposite of love is indifference

You made me believe
I had to be perfect
to be loved.

The moon taught me
there is beauty
in darkness too,
that even when
I don't feel whole,
I am enough.

I had a dream you
put your hand on my shoulder,
turned into a vampire,
and bit my neck.
I woke up to the sound
of my own shrieking.

When he tells you
he's a bad man,
believe him.

Reoccurring Dream

My grandmother asked me why I didn't want to go to bed. *I don't want to dream*, I told her. She said, *If you tell me, you won't see those bad dreams anymore.* I told her about the man with green eyes that kept chasing me. I never saw him again.

They try to hide,
but it always
gives them away—
cold eyes.

The cold hurts my bones,
cracks my knuckles
to the point of bleeding—
but this chill is nothing
compared to you.

I find myself
around the same
toxic people
with different faces
over
and over again.
I look up—
what is the lesson?

-stand up for yourself

#metoo

I never wished ill
on anybody,
but I prayed for your death.

God answered me
with a question,
Marine, what do you want?

Justice, I replied,
and He reminded me
who The Judge is.

In my sleep,
I release
toxic energy—
I release you.

I grew up hearing about my aunts' husbands beating them,
heard stories about their plans to leave,
heard family members say they don't understand
why my aunts weren't thankful for their husbands who provided.
For years I stayed quiet when boys and men put their hands on me.
For years I thought this behavior was normal.
Because it was normal in my world.
But it won't be anymore.

-Time's Up

The Day After My Aunt Haykush's Funeral

I went to Grandma's for lunch. She heated up yesterday's red rice and ground beef. *I already had fish,* she said, *but I'll sit with you. Are you making tea, Grandma? No, coffee,* she said. *I'll never forgive her husband. She lived in so much fear, it killed her. If you ever have problems when you get married, come share with me, I'll help you. It's not worth getting married and being afraid to live. It would've been better had she stayed home.* We cried, stared off into the living room, and drank the bitter coffee.

Dear Aunt Haykush,

I was thinking about you today. I was thinking I hope there's literature in heaven for you. I was remembering Grandma tell me you were the smart one. You were going to leave Armenia to study in England, but she didn't let you—you got married instead. I hope there's a mansion for you. I hope you get to study everything you ever wanted to. I hope you have peace and that you're happy. I hope you're able to guide your sons from up there. I hope you know how loved you are.

The heaviest pain
I've seen
in a man's eyes—
regret.

This year, I watched men bury my aunt,
watched them bury my nineteen-year-old cousin,
watched you fall in love.

In my room, there's nowhere to stand—
I can't find anything anymore.

I write at the darkest hours of the night
because I can't sleep
I can't sleep
I can't sleep
you have me up
thinking
thinking
thinking
of nothing
but something
but what if something
what if nothing
you have me up
you have me up
you have me

-anxiety

Some days I just want to run
until it hurts,
until the physical burn
overpowers all the feelings
I don't know what to do with.

The Morning Grandpa Sarkis Died

My twin cousins are three years old. Little Gevo woke up crying.
They were whispering secret things to each other. Their mother
was showing them family photos to distract them—*look at Grandpa
Sarkis*, little Avo said, *he's such a beautiful man.*

Every day feels like a week.
Dozens of relatives visit
wearing black.
They bring pastries, coffee, food.
I've lost count
of how many cups
of bitter Armenian coffee I've served,
how many cups of hot water
I've boiled for tea,
how many pastries I've eaten.
My body aches with grief,
and even the naps
in between seeing guests
don't give me the rest I need.

—*the mourning*

The Viewing

I couldn't look at my grandfather
in the open casket
his limp arms folded across
his torso
his made-up face
that didn't look like his face—
I couldn't look at the body
that didn't carry my grandfather anymore.

They say children
see angels
of loved ones that died.

The day after the funeral,
my 3-year-old cousin
looked up and said,

It's Grandpa—
he's playing with his toys,
at his house—

he's happy.
Hours later,
he pointed to the door,

smiled and said,
Grandpa left.

40 Days of Mourning

When someone dies
in an Armenian family,
there's forty days of mourning—
no celebrations
no colorful clothes
no dancing.
But if Easter comes
before the 40 days,
it is finished.

Easter is my favorite holiday—
each year, I am reminded
no matter what I face,
no matter the loss or devastation,
or dreams yet to be fulfilled,
there's a hope that endures
for eternity—
Jesus Christ rose
and defied death once and for all.

They Carry the Dead

They come back for them,
these little ants
with no eyes
and no feet.
They find the dead by their scent,
they come back
and carry the bodies—
the bodies that are the same size
as their own—
I would give my eyes and feet
to be an ant for a day,
to come back to your scent,
to carry you away.

Things aren't always
as they seem—
Jesus had to die
to rise from the grave.

The darkness doesn't
stand a chance
against the sun.

The Light

The very first creation. Light breaks through the darkness.

And gives us hope.

You are constant,
you never change,
it's nice to know
I can count on something
that always burns with light.

-The Sun

Sometimes I feel like a fly—
I wander aimlessly,
bump into walls
as I search for the light.

Yesterday evening as I was getting ready for bed, I was frustrated at the fly zipping around in my bathroom, making noise. Then, I paused for a second and watched it fly. Watched it bump into walls and mirrors, aimlessly. Watched its relentless pursuit of the light. And I thought, you and I are not that different, Fly. You and I are not that different.

Tell the Stories

The devil says, *If you speak*
you'll lose everything—
your family, your friends—
nobody will like you.
But God says,
Open your mouth
and speak!
Tell the stories of
your ancient ancestors,
your grandparents' struggles,
your lost childhood
and your survival.

I feel your energy around me
it wants to keep me small
it wants to shut me up
but my voice is thunder
and my light is the sun.

Sometimes I feel like I'm holding
my breath
like I'm underwater—
when I was seven,
I slipped below the water,
I couldn't swim,
I thought it was the end
I saw the light—
I have never felt as much
peace
as I did in that moment.

I watched *The Joan of Arc* as a child. I watched her suffer, stand up for her beliefs. She saw the clouds move, the skies open. I watched her wait as she talked to God. And I knew one day, I too would see the skies open.

If I could go back to my five-year-old self,
I'd tell her, you're not a burden. You're loved
more than you'll ever know. Don't stop praying.
God hears you. He will answer your prayers.

If I could go back to my sixteen-year-old self,
I'd tell her, you're stronger than you think you are.
You're valuable. If people don't see that, they don't
belong in your life. You are a poet. Don't ever forget that.

If I could go back to my twenty-one-year-old self, I'd tell
her, be patient. Keep working hard. Dream big. Forgive
and let go. You deserve to be happy. You're loved more
than you'll ever know. Don't stop praying, God hears you.

King of Kings

He has answered prayers from my childhood.
He paved roads on unmarked territories
for my ancestors to escape persecution
and find freedom.

When I was lost
He showed me who I am,
showed me the next steps to take
and gave me the strength to rise again.

And when I thought I lost it all,
He showed me He was removing
the toxic people that don't belong,
and that if I was left with less
but still had Him,
then I'd have everything.

So go ahead
tell me you're a proud atheist
tell me about your troubles
and talk to me of your pain.

And I'll tell you of the One
who changes the hearts of kings
with His justice
and with His love.

I had a dream of myself on Earth—
saw myself become smaller,
saw Earth become smaller,
realized how short our lives are
and how important eternity is.

In my dream,
I was praying in tongues,
casting off evil spirits.
I saw the hands of the devil
trying to get a grip on me,
I saw the hands of God
holding the whole Earth.

Love is the strongest
force in the world—
the reason God created
everything.

In the Park

My Father smiles,
runs across the park,
lifts me up
and twirls me around.
I hold on tight
as the curls swing
away from my face.
Look, he says,
pointing to the crescent moon—
I made that for you.

I am the moon—
I rise in the dark
to give you light.

In the Deep End

You can tread the shallow waters,
dip your toes to feel the temperature,
you can let them wash over your feet
again and again.

You can stand
and watch your life pass you by,
like the Swiss trains—
every hour, by the hour.

You can complain that God doesn't
hear you, or love you—
you can stand still
when He's telling you to move!

But it's in the deep end where God showed me
the darkness in my own heart—
it's in the deep end when I prayed for
the death of my oppressors,

He taught me what forgiveness really means—
70x7 times, He tells us to forgive.
It's in the deep end He showed me
how much more they suffer

for causing suffering onto others.
In the deep end, He taught me
to have compassion on them.
He humbled me

because God opposes the proud.
He showed me that riches
will never buy happiness

because only love can do that.

Only God can do that, because He is love.
So you can tread the shallow waters,
let them wash over your feet again and again.
But it's only in the deep end, where you will find God.

If I knew things could
be this different,
I would go back,
I would forgive you sooner.

Mixed Dreams

1.

I walk up to my doctor at his office and hug him. I sit on a chair in my gown, and wait for him. He asks me to wash his dishes at the apartment I grew up in. There are rows of clean cups. He stands beside me, watching, with crossed arms.

2.

I sit across from my pastors. I don't remember what we talk about. Eggs crack on the couches.

3.

In the office, a colleague says she wants an abortion. She's in her second trimester.

4.

I wake up. There's a newborn girl laying in a car seat. Her eyes are still closed. My sister picks her up. Then I pick her up. *We have to leave,* she says. *Hold on,* I say, *I just want to hold her a little longer.*

I am not a mother yet.
Sometimes I wonder
if I'll have a boy or a girl.

I see children everywhere—
watch mothers chase their sons,
walk hand in hand with their daughters.

I help my aunt take care of her twin boys,
but when I hold a baby girl,
only she and I exist.

To My Future Children

I love you already,
so when you are born,
you will know it.

The skin on my face
is peeling—
my entire being
is shedding the old
shedding the old
shedding the old,
making way for the new.

All the cells in our bodies
are destroyed and replaced
every seven years—
it took four times
for this metamorphosis
to occur,
for me to realize,
self-love is what will save me.

The strife, hostility, and conflict
clouded my judgment—
I couldn't tell
if I was an enemy or an ally
in the war waged
inside my head—
I raised the white flag
when I decided to live life
on my own terms.

I used to fold my arms
close to my body
wherever I stood,
tried to take as little
space as possible,
I'd shrivel to one side
of the bed each evening,
even when I danced
I would stay in small spaces.
Fear made me want to hide,
but its time has come—
I wasn't made to live small.

That heavy feeling in the pit of my stomach
that weighs me down,
that makes it hard to breathe,
the critic on my shoulder that questions
my every move,
that questions my worth,
all left when I replaced your voice
with mine.

I look in the mirror—
it was you
I was waiting for
this whole time.

I learned how strong soft is,
because the softer I get,
the stronger I become.

I wonder who I was in a past life
that gave me this strength.

I am the messenger
of my ancestors.

All the women
that came before me
paved a part of the path
through what they suffered,
they gave me the vision
to remove bars and boundaries
that kept women small
for so long,
when it is us women
who create the earth.

The Soul

The very essence of our being. Our core. Our truest selves.

God created souls. And gave us bodies to live on Earth.

Young and Beautiful

I don't want to be
young forever—
I want to see my changing face.

I want to see my belly grow
a human being,
watch her leave my body.

I don't want to be young forever.
I want to be friends with my mother—
share stories we never could.

I want her to sing to my daughters,
teach them to cook *dolma*, prepare a table,
and tell them about Armenia.

Armenia

I want to touch your ancient architecture.
I want to run in your green gardens,
swim in the *Sevan*,
pick up your soil,
and hold You in my hands.

I want to feel the natural springs of *Jermug*
in my mouth, eat your sweet grapes,
and drink the juice of your pomegranates.
I want to travel on your unpaved roads,
and see your desolate cities.

I want to dance and sing with your people,
to walk, sit and eat with them,
listen to their stories,
laugh, and cry with them.

I'm a daughter of
Armenian immigrants,
thankful to be born
in this free country,
that will never feel like home.

Home

When my mom found out that her mother had a brain tumor, she flew
to Armenia. She hadn't been back in ten years. I was seven, and cried,
I want to go too! But she said, *You don't know what you want—you can't
shower there every day, the bathrooms are outside, the milk doesn't taste the same—
you wouldn't like it.* But even before she brought back a photo of the cottage
she had grown up in, I knew she was wrong.

Ancestors

I carry you in my heart—
I carry all of you
who couldn't speak,
couldn't dream,
couldn't live.

Genocide, 1915

1.

When I dream about my family in Armenia, I see images of death.

2.

A woman once told me that the effects of trauma can pass from
generation to generation.

3.

In Armenia, men kidnapped women to marry. That's how my great aunt
got married. When my mother was single, they said she was too picky.
I'm afraid to be alone.

4.

I was so anxious, I broke out in hives. I asked my pastor to pray for my
skin. He prayed, *Lord, take away the harshness that has come to Marine and
her people.*

Diaspora

My grandmother is an American citizen now.
She was born in Syria after the Armenian Genocide,
but I don't know how her family got there.

I don't know if her parents fled during the genocide,
or if they were exiled
and forced into the Syrian deserts by the Turks.

I'm not sure if her father
survived the genocide
or how or where he died.

But I remember my grandmother's mother.
She was tall, obese, and had ten kids.
She never talked.

I asked my mother how her grandparents got to Syria,
but she doesn't know, and I've never asked
my grandmother—I don't want her to remember.

Conversations with Grandma and Her Siblings

I never asked my grandmother
about the story of our family's survival.
But when my grandfather died,
she and her siblings started talking about
their grandfather.
How he saw his parents and oldest brother
dead under a tree, from starvation.
How his other brother got lost.
And their grandpa was taken by a nomad family
who couldn't have children of their own.
By chance or the grace of God,
my great-great grandfather survived a genocide
and gave generations of descendants
strength, resilience, and the will to live.

The Aftermath

They took our land,
they took our churches,
they devastated ancient architectures—
holy land and temples of worship,
they took our people,
they took our peace,
they buried millions
of Armenians
that reunited with the soil,
only to be planted
to grow again—
stronger, more perseverant,
and blooming
on every continent.

When one Armenian meets another,
in the diaspora,
it's always a joyous event.
Like long-lost neighbors
reuniting in a foreign land—
it's a taste of home.

Today is my grandmother's birthday—
Grandma why are you so sad?
I always used to ask her.

Now, I just want to make her smile—
I'll never understand what she had to survive
so that I can have life.

Armenian American

My Armenian family and friends
don't understand how I live so boldly—
I don't follow the ancient rulebook
that governs their lives.

Immigrants and Americans
always ask me where I'm from—
Glendale, California I say,
No, they say, *where are you really from?*

Alas, it's the blood of the ancients
that runs through my veins—
the trauma and generosity,
the loss yet strength,
the love of dance—
it's the sound of the *duduk*
that flows through me.

The Armenian language
is an ancient art—
not many will understand
the techniques of its artists,
their choices of color,
or its surreal nature,
but it's the most beautiful gallery
for every Armenian.

My father's father was a painter.
He died young—
I never got to meet the man
that gave my dad the gift of art.
But I see him in every painting,
I see him in every photograph,
every dance—
I see him through the kindness
in my father's eyes.

In the Living Room

Our father set up
his lights, his umbrellas
and backdrop,
so my sister and I
could pose in ballet
skirts and slippers.
But when he left,
we took turns
taking each other's pictures,
put on tulle veils
and pretended to be brides.

Armenian Wedding

The tables are full
of barbequed meat,
potatoes, rice,
dolmas, tabuleh,
and hummus.
There is wine,
tequila, whiskey
and champagne.
The band plays
drums and
an Armenian flute
outside the home
of the groom,
and outside
the home of the bride,
while relatives dance
and take over
the sidewalks,
the streets,
and the new
in-laws exchange
gifts in embroidered
handmade baskets.

Exchanges with my Grandpa

Our conversations are always
the same. My grandfather asks
about school, I say it's fine.

We watch TV together. He turns
his head so he can see with his good eye
and hear with his good ear.

When I lean in to hug him,
he shakes my hand,
pats my shoulder.

He tells me,
consider and reconsider
before you marry.

They tell me I need to get married
but they don't know
I hold my grandmothers' traumas
in my body—
my father's mother was given away
in marriage to her brother's friend.
I didn't think my father would
give him my hand, she told me,
I didn't want to marry him.
And my mother's mother
was fifteen when she married
my grandpa who was thirty.
I'd try to bite him
when he came near me, she said,
I'd bite him as hard as I could.

The Taboos of Armenian Culture

You can't talk about miscarriages
you can't talk about infertility,
infidelity, or abortions—
I found out in my twenties that Armenia
has the second highest rate
of female abortions in the world.
You can't talk about periods
can't talk about sex
can't talk about domestic abuse
or mental health
about how all these topics
are taboo,
and if you're a woman,
you just can't talk.

I will speak for
my aunts and ancestors
who couldn't speak
without worry
of being beaten.

You don't know someone
until you've walked a mile
in their skin,
listened to the music
of their ancestors,
until you've tasted
the bitterness of breaking
their cultural norms.

Broken glass taught me
there is something so beautiful
in shattering.

Ancestors 2

You thought mourning
was the only way to live—
I will find joy,
lift my arms to the heavens,
and share it with you.

I met my aunt Khatun for the first time
when she visited from Russia.

She gave me a clock—it had a peacock on it
with blue and green feathers and gold jewels.

I didn't know who I was bringing this for, she said,
but when I saw the colors in your room,

I knew it was yours. Each time you look at it,
may you know you're closer to your dreams.

Ancestors 3

You are my angels
guiding me
to truth,
to joy,
to freedom you never had.